Dealing with Grief and How to Move Beyond It - Companion Guide

Keia K. Holt

Other books by Keia Holt:

Dealing with Grief and How to Move Beyond It
ISBN: 979-8-9990346-0-1 Paperback
ISBN: 979-8-9990346-1-8 eBook
ISBN: 979-8-9990346-2-5 Hardcover

Sermon Notebook and Journal
ISBN: 979-8-9990346-6-3 Paperback

This Journal Belongs To:

My Beginning Date of Healing:

Table of Contents

About this Journal

This journal can be used in conjunction with the book, "**Dealing with Grief and How to Move Beyond It,**" or used independently. Just like the book, I created this journal to help others with their grief. I have experienced long-term grief, unexpected grief, and relationship grief. But I consciously chose not to allow the grief to take over my life or prevent me from living a fruitful life. I pray that you make the same decision. This journal contains encouragement, questions/prompts to consider, and bible verses for encouragement.

You can purchase the book on Amazon or get a signed copy from www.keiaholt.com.

I am praying for your healing. Please remember that there is joy and healing on the other side of grief.

How to Use this Journal

You are in control. You can use this journal every day (I recommend this for those who are in active grief). Or you can use this journal on the days when your grief is stronger than others, you need some encouragement, or you are ready to process your feelings.

Look at the **Table of Contents**. You can, but don't have to use this journal in order; it's effective either way. You can pick the topic that is most applicable for that day.

The best way to process grief is to acknowledge it and the feelings associated with it. Journaling is one great way to do this.

In this journal, you will see many challenges and things to ponder, or to help you through this grieving process. You will also see self-assessments to help you gauge your progress.

Understand that the goal is not to remain in a state of grief. We know that as long as we keep living, we will experience loss in many different ways (death of a loved one, death of a relationship, death of a pet, loss of a job or house...).

The book, "**Dealing with Grief and How to Move Beyond It**," is me telling my story of grief (loss of parents, relationship, and grandmothers). But since it was published in July 2025, others have shared how it helped them process other types of grief, too. With that in mind, I wanted to incorporate some of those topics and feedback.

Benefits of Journaling

- Journaling helps to process your emotions (grief, anger, sadness, joy).

- Seeing your thoughts on paper can help bring clarity to your situation.

- Writing things down can help you remember (it could be a new scripture, your new mantra, or quotes to help you process your emotions).

- Journaling is good for healing and self-development. I recommend adding a date to your entries so you can see your progress when you look back on this time.

- Journaling is a way to assess your progress when you read your older entries.

- **Suggestion:** Try writing for 15 to 30 minutes a day for three to four days, or as long as a week if you feel writing continues to be helpful. You could also try writing for 15 to 30 minutes once a week for a month. Some research on journaling says that that writing has stronger effects when it extends over more days.*

*https://www.health.harvard.edu/mind-and-mood/writing-to-ease-grief

The Butterfly

Butterflies have four stages of metamorphosis: egg, larva, pupa, and adult.

Egg

Eggs are laid on plants by the adult female butterfly. These plants will then become the food for the hatching caterpillars.

Caterpillar: The Feeding Stage

The next stage is the larva. This is also called a caterpillar if the insect is a butterfly or a moth.

Pupa: The Transition Stage

When the caterpillar is full grown and stops eating, it becomes a pupa. The pupa of butterflies is also called a chrysalis.

Adult: The Reproductive Stage

The adult stage is what most people think of when they think of butterflies. They look very different from the larva. The caterpillar has a few tiny eyes, stubby legs and very short antennae. The adults have long legs, long antennae, and compound eyes. They can also fly by using their large and colorful wings. The one thing they can't do is grow.*

*According to The Academy of Natural Sciences of Drexel University, September 3, 2025, https://ansp.org/exhibits/online-exhibits/butterflies/lifecycle/.

The Butterfly on the Cover

The difference between the stages of grief and the metamorphosis of the butterfly is that a butterfly's transition is linear, and the timing of the butterfly's change is known. Our grief is not linear. It is not timed, and it is not always the same. Grief can be different with each death. The third experience with loss may not hurt as much as the first loss. That doesn't mean that you love that person less; it's just that you're learning how to deal with grief.

When you look at the picture of the butterfly in its different stages, it isn't pretty. But each stage has a purpose, and it is important for the egg, larva, and pupa to make it to the next stage.

That's just like dealing with your grief. It isn't pretty, but it is purposeful. The emphasis is not about being beautiful at the end but about surviving to the end, striving for the time to spread your wings and fly.

Inhale . . . Exhale . . . Breathe! You are alive! Now live!

How Are You Feeling?

How are you feeling? Are you angry, hurt, depressed, or confused? How is your relationship with Jesus Christ? Do you find comfort in the scriptures? Are you reaching out to friends for comfort? Are you praying for strength? How are you feeling? Add a date to your response and look back later to see if your answers have changed as you progress through this journal.

What is Grief?

Grief is defined as "keen mental suffering or distress over affliction or loss; sharp sorrow; painful regret," according to Dictionary.com. Grief is usually associated with the loss of a loved one. But grief can be caused by many things including divorce, losing or changing jobs, moving, change in financial status, broken friendships, loss of faith, or the death of a pet.*

"Grief is a reaction to loss, and like a fingerprint, it is different for everyone."* When we lose someone we love, we experience grief, mourning, and bereavement. These are similar terms, but they have different meanings. **Grief** is our reaction to a loss. Just like each person is unique, the way we grieve them will be unique as well.

Mourning is how we express our grief in public. Mourning practices differ amongst various cultures, religions, and regions of the world. In the Bible, people would mourn by tearing their clothes, wearing sackcloth, and covering themselves in ashes (for examples, see Genesis 37:34; Esther 4:1; Job 2:8).

Bereavement refers to that specific period of mourning. People often take bereavement leave from work after the death of a loved one. They set aside time to grieve and take care of the needs that arise after the loss of a loved one, like funeral arrangements, finances, and to meet the needs of their family.

*Asma Rehman, "How Long Does the Grieving Process Last?" accessed February 26, 2025, https://www.griefrecoveryhouston.com/how-long-does-grieving-process-last/.

*"What is grief?" (written September 24, 2024) accessed April 5, 2025, https://hospicefoundation.org/what-is-grief/.

The Five Stages of Grief

Elisabeth Kübler-Ross introduced the five stages of grief in her book, On Death and Dying, which have now become widely accepted: <u>denial, anger, bargaining, depression, and acceptance</u>. These stages help us process loss and adapt successfully to changes in our realities. We don't all experience all five stages, nor do we process each stage the same way. Some stages last longer than others, and it's perfectly normal to revisit stages.

It is important to work your way through whichever stage you are feeling. There aren't any shortcuts to moving beyond grief, and there aren't any time limits. Some stages might be shorter than others, while others may last longer. Remember, there aren't many rules when you're dealing with grief. But do not self-medicate or do harmful things to yourself. It may feel like a relief at the time, but it's a temporary solution with permanent consequences.

There is Power in the Words of Jesus

John 11 tells the story about Lazarus and his two sisters, Mary and Martha. Lazarus was sick. The sisters sent a message to Jesus and asked Him to come to them. Jesus said, "Lazarus's sickness will not end in death. No, it happened for the glory of God so that the Son of God will receive glory from this." After two days, Jesus told the disciples that it was time to return to Judea. Lazarus had "fallen asleep," and Jesus was going to wake him.

By the time He arrived, Lazarus had been dead for four days and was in the grave. Martha told Jesus that if He had come sooner, Lazarus would not have died. Jesus told her that she would see her brother again. Martha agreed, but it would be in the resurrection. Jesus said, "I am the resurrection and the life. Anyone who believes in me will live, even after dying. Everyone who lives in me and believes in me will never ever die. Do you believe this, Martha?" She stated that she did and went to get her sister, Mary. Mary fell at Jesus's feet and told Him that if He had been there, her brother would not have died.

Both sisters understood that Jesus had the power to heal the sick. They were His friends; they didn't understand why Jesus did not come sooner to save Lazarus.

We may find ourselves in this same situation. Have you ever thought, "God, why didn't you heal my loved one? God, I had faith that you could do it; I don't understand why you didn't."

Why did Jesus delay His return by two days? To show everyone the power and glory of God, and so that others may believe. **John 11:40-43** Jesus responded, "Didn't I tell you that you would see God's glory if you believe?" So they rolled the stone aside. Then Jesus looked up to heaven and said, "Father, thank you for hearing me. You always hear me, but I said it out loud for the sake of all these people standing here, so that they will believe you sent me." Then Jesus shouted, "Lazarus, come out!"

We may never understand why God heals some people and allows others to die. But we cannot let God's response affect our faith. He is still God, whether He chooses to heal on earth or in heaven!

Trade Your Beauty for Ashes
Isaiah 61:1-3

The Spirit of the Sovereign LORD is upon me, for the LORD has anointed me to bring good news to the poor.
He has sent me to comfort the brokenhearted and to proclaim that captives will be released and prisoners will be freed.

He has sent me to tell those who mourn that the time of the LORD's favor has come, and with it, the day of God's anger against their enemies.

To all who mourn in Israel, he will give a crown of beauty for ashes, a joyous blessing instead of mourning, festive praise instead of despair.

In their righteousness, they will be like great oaks that the LORD has planted for his own glory.

———————

At the right time, God will come along and exchange your ashes for beauty because that season of your life has ended. Let them go and embrace what lies ahead.

How I Will Release My Ashes and Embrace Beauty

Dealing with Grief

Dealing with grief is kind of like exercise; you must do it for yourself. I am more faithful when I have a workout partner. So, consider this Companion Guide your partner. Please don't be afraid to reach out for help through a counselor or group therapy. It really does make a difference to speak with people who understand how you're feeling.

In order to move beyond grief, we must deal with it first. There is not a timeline for grief, but "the American Psychological Association (APA) defines grief as lasting from six months to two years. Symptoms gradually improve as time passes."* Although there are some commonalities to dealing with grief, everyone's response to grief is different.

You may find yourself replaying conversations that you had with a loved one and wishing that it had gone differently. Unfortunately, we cannot change that. And it just brings guilt and sorrow that cannot be rectified. You might even feel like you wish you had told them that you loved them one more time. They knew that you loved them.

After my father's death, I realized that he was there for me with all the other deaths and the breakup; now he was gone. Who was going to help me get through his death? I came to the realization that God was there with me through all the deaths and the breakup, too. And God would be the one to help me get

*"Grief," reviewed February 22, 2023, accessed March 27, 2025, https://my.clevelandclinic.org/health/diseases/24787-grief.

through my father's death. **Deuteronomy 31:8** *Do not be afraid or discouraged, for the LORD will personally go ahead of you. He will be with you; he will neither fail you nor abandon you."*

Acceptance does not always come with understanding. We may never understand why a person died when they did. But this is where our faith in God must override that mindset. I cannot explain why some people die young and others get to live to be octogenarians. I cannot explain why my mother was struck with cancer in her early twenties. But I have learned to accept these facts and then find a way to deal with it.

One time, I was speaking to my nephew Rasheed. I pointed to the entertainment center. I indicated the biggest square and then pointed to the smaller sections. I told him that he had to learn to keep the most important things in the big square and learn to move other things to the smaller sections. I was explaining what it means to compartmentalize. That's the same thing with grief. When grief is new, it's in the biggest square of our lives. It is all that we can focus on. However, as we progress through the stages of grief, the size of the square representing our grief should change.

And, prayerfully, your grief continues moving until it's in the smallest square of your life. It's not gone; it's still there, but it's not so prevalent.

Dealing with the Effects of Grief

Every day won't be easy, but you will overcome your grief if you acknowledge it and then deal with it. How has grief affected your life? Are you avoiding people, places, or things? Did you stop socializing? Are you sad most days? How do you feel?

God, You Are Not Enough!

This chapter was in response to a conversation that I had with one of my best friends. Her mother was exhibiting signs of dementia. She started to say that she didn't know what she would do without---I cut her off and did not let her finish her statement. I told her that to say that she cannot live without her mother meant that she could not live without God. I told her that she was saying, "God, you are not enough!"

Anyone who declares that they cannot live without their loved one is telling God that He is not enough for you to keep living. You may say what she said, "That's not what I meant." But if you decide that you cannot live without someone or something, that's exactly what you're saying. It's ok to be mad about what's going on, but don't you dare give up on life!

Denial is the initial period after a loss in which the grieving person does not accept the reality of the loss.

Sometimes, the way to deal with grief at this stage is to deny that it's happening or has happened. Some examples of denial are:

- "I don't want to talk about it; it's not real."
- "I didn't see their body, so I don't believe it."
- "He/she wasn't sick enough to die!"

Coming out of the denial stage is a blessing; it's a sign that you're on the path to healing. And you may not feel like it, but you're getting stronger emotionally. "Denial allows you time to adjust to who you are, where you are, and what your next step will be following a loss."*

As you transition out of the denial stage, you may experience new emotions that were suppressed before, like sorrow.* That is normal.

* Iris Waichler, "Denial Stage of Grief: Examples, What to Expect, & How to Cope," accessed June 1, 2025, https://www.choosingtherapy.com/denialstage-of-grief.

* Kimberly Holland, "The Stages of Grief and What to Expect," accessed February 3, 2025, http://healthline.com/health/stages-of-grief#5-stages.

My Feelings about Denial

Anger is rational and irrational at the same time. It is a rational feeling after losing a loved one, but the anger is irrational because it is often misplaced. "Where denial may be considered a coping mechanism, anger is a masking effect. Anger is hiding many of the emotions and pain you carry."* We may mask anger by redirecting anger toward ourselves, our deceased loved ones, family members, doctors, or even God. This kind of anger can be unpredictable and hurtful.

Some examples of anger are:
- "Why didn't he/she take better care of themselves?"
- "God, if you were real, you wouldn't let my loved one die!"
- "God, if you loved me, you would save my loved one."
- "I think the doctor did something. He/she didn't care about my loved one."

For those who may be comforting someone who is grieving, you may hear, "No one is helping me. No one knows what I'm going through. No one understands. No one, no one, no one!" This can be very hurtful to hear when you are the "no one" who has been helping. But we must remember that the anger stage is not the rational stage. Don't take it personally; it's just their anger speaking.

*Kimberly Holland, "The Stages of Grief and What to Expect," accessed February 3, 2025, http://healthline.com/health/stages-of-grief#5-stages.

Are you feeling angry? Do you have regrets about some things that you said or did? Are there events that angered or frustrated you? Release that anger by writing it down.

Bargaining is a way of coping when you feel helpless. Death is happening and we cannot do anything about it. "One of the most compelling is the bargaining stage of grief—a time during which an individual struggles to comprehend how to accept the loss of a loved one, possession, job, or something else."* We begin wondering what could have been done differently, wishing there was a way to change the outcome. Guilt seems to be a part of the bargaining stage. But just because we feel guilty does not mean that we are; remember, feelings aren't always rational.

Some examples of bargaining are:

- "I should have demanded that the doctors do more."
- "Maybe if I had treated him/her better, this wouldn't have happened."
- "God if you heal (or save) my loved one, I'll start (or stop) _____."

*Theresa Lupcho, "What is the bargaining stage of grief? How to understand and work through the bargaining process after experiencing loss," accessed June 1, 2025, https://thriveworks.com/help-with/grief-loss/what-is-the-bargaining-stage-of-grief.

Have You Ever Found Yourself Bargaining with God?

You might feel out of control because you cannot physically do anything to heal your loved one or bring them back. So what can you do to get beyond this feeling?

Depression can cause one to feel sad and hopeless after the loss of a loved one. During this period, you may withdraw from people and your usual schedule. You may spend more time sleeping; you may neglect your self-care. You may need to seek some additional help to deal with your grief, and that's OK. Remember that grief is like a fingerprint—it is unique to each person, and the effects of each death on you can be different, too. And multiple deaths close together can trigger depression.

Some examples of the depression stage are:
- "I'm going to quit (insert activity). It won't be fun without my loved one."
- "I can't live without my loved one."
- "I can get through this on my own."
- "I'll never be happy again."

My Thoughts on Depression

How will you guard yourself against depression? Or if you're dealing with it, how do you plan to overcome it?

Acceptance is coming to the realization that your loved one is physically gone and they are not coming back. Acceptance does not mean that you're happy your loved one is gone, but you have acknowledged it and accepted that they are. Now you must figure out how to live your life without their presence while holding on to their memory.

Dr. Judy Ho says that the stages of grief are more circular than linear.* "For example, you may feel like you've accepted the loss, then something happens months later, and you circle back to denial. That's a very natural and realistic way of thinking— don't feel like you're taking steps back."* I can attest that: as I processed my mother's impending death, there were times that I cycled back to denial. I just couldn't believe she didn't get better this time. This is how some people deal with grief, and it is normal.

Some examples from the acceptance stage are:
- "God, I miss my loved one, but I know that you will help me to heal."
- "I accept that my loved one is gone; I know that they aren't suffering anymore. I take comfort in that."
- "It's OK for me to live my life. That's what they would want me to do."

*Alyssa Jung, "How to Deal With Grief After Suffering a Painful Loss, According to Mental Health Experts," published February 15, 2021, accessed March 27, 2025, https://www.prevention.com/health/mental-health/a35379156/how-to-deal-with-grief/?utm_source=google&utm_medium=cpc&utm_campaign=mgu_ga_pre_md_pmx_hybd_mix_us_20739785489&gad_source=1&gclid=Cj0KCQjwqIm_BhDnARIsAKBYcmsrzb62wQ0nABA8vmcipU4RAjXlSRSRKqDv11o-hGMD6hceqHrfi7oaAkxhEALw_wcB.

My Plan for Acceptance

How will I get to the acceptance stage? Write what acceptance looks like to you and steps to help you get there (friends/family, prayer, grief support...).

A Prayer for Angry Days

It's hard to understand why some people are healed while others die. Let's be honest, it can cause someone to be angry. "Why did my loved one have to die? Why couldn't my loved one be saved?" It feels unfair that your loved one died while others didn't. These are open and honest feelings. And you aren't the first person who has felt this way.

Unfortunately, we may never understand God's ways. He even tells us that in **Isaiah 55:8-9**. By faith, we must accept that our God does not make mistakes, even when we don't understand His ways. **Proverbs 3:5-7** *Trust in the LORD with all your heart; do not depend on your own understanding. Seek his will in all you do, and he will show you which path to take.*

Sometimes our anger is rooted in fear. There may be fear of living life without your loved one. It is realizing that your identity has changed now that your loved one is gone. And being angry about all of it! The pain and anger that you feel are an expression of the amount of love that you had for your loved one. **2 Timothy 1:7** *For God has not given us a spirit of fear and timidity, but of power, love, and self-discipline.*

Let's pray:
Father, I am angry and hurting right now. I really miss my loved one, and I don't understand why he/she had to die. But I trust in you, God. I trust you to calm my fears, to remove my anger, and to give me peace. Father, please help me to accept their death. Please help me to hold on to their memory and live my life without guilt. Amen.

Coming Closer to God

James 4:8 *Come close to God, and God will come close to you. Wash your hands, you sinners; purify your hearts, for your loyalty is divided between God and the world.*

Do you have a desire to be closer to God? Don't allow grief to make you turn away from God or cause you to give up on God.

God always desires a relationship with us. Instead of letting grief push you away, make an intentional decision to draw closer to God.

○ Trusting fully – Relying on God's strength, wisdom, and love rather than your own understanding.

○ Staying close spiritually – Through prayer, meditation, worship, and reading sacred texts.

○ Seeking God's guidance – Turning to God for direction in choices and life's challenges.

○ Remaining faithful – Even when life feels overwhelming, confusing, or painful.

○ Letting go of control – Surrendering your fears, plans, and anxieties to God.

Grief is Personal

People do not always grieve the same way. Yes, there are documented stages of grief that are common to most people. But whether someone experiences all five stages varies. The length of time in each stage is different. Grief is personal.

You can have siblings who lose a parent, and they may not grieve the same way. Parents who lose a child, may not grieve the same way. Grief is personal.

As long as you are dealing with your grief and learning how to move beyond it in a healthy way, you are doing GREAT! How have you experienced differences in processing your grief?

_____

_____

_____

_____

_____

_____

_____

_____

_____

_____

_____

My Metamorphosis

I am changing from grieving to ...

Subtraction

As I lost family members, I felt like my life was full of subtraction. I lost them, one by one; death was slowly subtracting from my family. It was a painful time in my life.

While I was experiencing those deaths, I didn't see them as "subtractions," but when I started writing the book, the realization hit me with jarring clarity. I even wrote a poem called "Subtraction" and put it in the book. That was just one of the many revelations that I came to while writing the book.

I was encouraged by the fact that although I lost three people in one year, I didn't crumble. I hurt, I cried, I was angry, I grieved, but I didn't die. By the grace of God, I made it through the other side of my grief. My prayer is that you do, too.

As long as we keep living, we will continue to lose friends and family. But we must find a way to deal with our grief without allowing it to overtake our lives.

My Subtractions

What subtractions have you experienced? It may not just be about those who died, but what other losses have you experienced?

_____

_____

_____

_____

_____

_____

_____

How do you plan to handle future subtractions from your life (unfortunately, it is inevitable)? Having a plan does not prevent grief, but having a plan helps one to deal with grief. Will you reach out for help; join a support group/therapy, journal, or speak with friends?

_____

_____

_____

_____

_____

_____

_____

The Roadblocks of Life

We all plan our lives out and hope that it goes just like that. Unfortunately, it rarely does.

The person that you pledged your undying love to suddenly tells you that they want a divorce.

A close friend gets sick and never recovers.

The pet that you've had for decades, that comforted you through so many difficult challenges in life, suddenly dies.

The person you planned to grow old with dies.

Bam, roadblock! When the path you were traveling on is no longer available, what will you do?

I turn to my Lord and Savior, Jesus Christ. He is my Comforter and my Redeemer. And He will be yours too, the moment that you invite Him into your situation.

Jeremiah 17:7 *But blessed are those who trust in the LORD and have made the LORD their hope and confidence.*

Dealing with Roadblocks

How will you handle the roadblocks of life? They will happen; they may have already happened. As long as we keep living, roadblocks will continue to come up. What's your plan for navigating them?

One Day at a Time

It's easy to get overwhelmed when you think about everything that needs to be done. It's as if life doesn't care that you're grieving. But take each day one day at a time. Focus on what you need to do TODAY. Maybe focus on getting through today, or maybe the next hour or the next minute. One - at – a - time.

At the end of each day, think about what you can do to prepare for the next day, only focusing on the major tasks for that day (not <u>everything</u> that needs to be done right now).

Doing simple things like preparing your lunch, setting out your clothes, and journaling can decrease your stress the next morning.

How I Will Prepare for Each Day

Scripture Encouragement

- **Matthew 6:34** *So don't worry about tomorrow, for tomorrow will bring its own worries. Today's trouble is enough for today.*

- **Romans 15:13** *I pray that God, the source of hope, will fill you completely with joy and peace because you trust in him. Then you will overflow with confident hope through the power of the Holy Spirit.*

- **Jeremiah 29:11** *For I know the plans I have for you," says the LORD. "They are plans for good and not for disaster, to give you a future and a hope."*

- **John 14:27** *"I am leaving you with a gift—peace of mind and heart. And the peace I give is a gift the world cannot give. So don't be troubled or afraid.*

- **Psalm 31:24** *So be strong and courageous, all you who put your hope in the LORD!*

- **Deuteronomy 31:6** *So be strong and courageous! Do not be afraid and do not panic before them. For the LORD your God will personally go ahead of you. He will neither fail you nor abandon you."*

- **Psalm 121:1-2** *I look up to the mountains— does my help come from there? My help comes from the LORD, who made heaven and earth!*

How the Scriptures Encourage Me

"Having a Tough Day"
Words of Encouragement

If I cry today, that is okay.

I miss (insert loved one's name), and that is okay.

It is ok not to be ok, for a while. But I must work towards being ok.

I know that I need to heal from my pain. Healing doesn't happen overnight. I will be patient with myself during the process.

Encourage Myself

1 Samuel 30:6 *David was now in great danger because all his men were very bitter about losing their sons and daughters, and they began to talk of stoning him. But David found strength in the LORD his God.* Feeling blue? Write about it. Expressing your feelings is a great way to deal with them.

A Prayer for Difficult Days

Heavenly Father, I need you right now. I am feeling sad, I miss my loved one, and I need You.

You said in **Psalm 34:18** that you are near the brokenhearted and that you save those crushed in spirit. Please come near me and save me.

You said in **Matthew 5:4** that those who mourn are blessed and will be comforted. Please comfort me.

In **Psalm 107:27**, you said that you will turn to the prayer of the destitute and will not despise their prayer. Lord, please turn to me and hear me, please do not despise my prayer.

In **Isaiah 26:3**, you said that you will keep us in perfect peace if we keep our minds stayed on you because we trust in you. Lord, I am here because I trust you, and I need your perfect peace!

Thank you, Lord, for hearing and answering my prayer. In Jesus's name, amen.

◆————————————◆

Matthew 11:28-30 NLT

Then Jesus said, "Come to me, all of you who are weary and carry heavy burdens, and I will give you rest. Take my yoke upon you. Let me teach you, because I am humble and gentle at heart, and you will find rest for your souls. For my yoke is easy to bear, and the burden I give you is light."

Dealing with Difficult Days

What is a healthy way for you to process your feelings?
What healthy coping techniques can you use?

_____

_____

_____

_____

_____

_____

_____

_____

_____

_____

_____

_____

_____

_____

_____

_____

_____

_____

Denial, Anger, Bargaining, Depression, Acceptance

Which of these emotions have you experienced? Did you repeat any of them? Are you intentionally working your way through the stages to get to the acceptance stage? How? And if not, why?

_____

_____

_____

_____

_____

_____

_____

_____

_____

_____

_____

_____

_____

_____

_____

_____

Comfort in Prayer

Does prayer decrease your anger? Does prayer comfort you? What are your favorite scriptures?

_____

_____

_____

_____

_____

_____

_____

_____

_____

_____

_____

_____

_____

_____

_____

_____

_____

Focusing on the Positive

When we're in the midst of our grief, we usually focus on all the negative things that are going on. People may not be reaching out with visits and calls the way that we'd like them to. Perhaps they meant to be comforting, but instead they said something infuriating. It may feel like everything is going wrong at the same time, and you can't control any of it.

My recommendation is to stop and take a breath. Take a mental assessment. What is going well? What have you maintained in spite of the loss? Yes, changes are going to happpen but they may not all be bad. It will be different, but it doesn't mean it will be bad.

Philippians 4:6-7 Don't worry about anything; instead, pray about everything. Tell God what you need, and thank him for all he has done. Then you will experience God's peace, which exceeds anything we can understand. His peace will guard your hearts and minds as you live in Christ Jesus.

Philippians 4:8 *And now, dear brothers and sisters, one final thing. Fix your thoughts on what is true, and honorable, and right, and pure, and lovely, and admirable. Think about things that are excellent and worthy of praise.*

"Focusing on the positive" is not about ignoring reality. Focusing on the positive instead of the negative is a stress reducer. Added stress takes a negative toll on our health, mood, and perspective.

Think on These Things

Philippians 4:8 *And now, dear brothers and sisters, one final thing. Fix your thoughts on what is true, and honorable, and right, and pure, and lovely, and admirable. Think about things that are excellent and worthy of praise.*

What are the positive things going on in your life right now? It can be a statement of gratefulness or your recognition of the good things that have remained, despite your loss.

Psalm 23

**1** The LORD is my shepherd; I have all that I need.

**2** He lets me rest in green meadows; he leads me beside peaceful streams.

**3** He renews my strength. He guides me along right paths, bringing honor to his name.

**4** Even when I walk through the darkest valley, I will not be afraid, for you are close beside me. Your rod and your staff protect and comfort me.

**5** You prepare a feast for me in the presence of my enemies. You honor me by anointing my head with oil. My cup overflows with blessings.

**6** Surely your goodness and unfailing love will pursue me all the days of my life, and I will live in the house of the LORD forever.

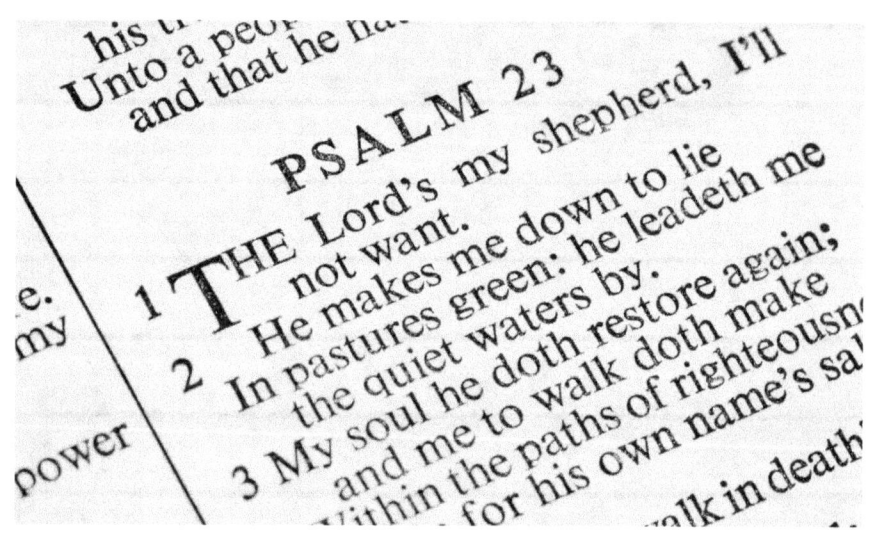

How the Lord is My Shepherd

Do you feel that the Lord is with you? Do you feel like He is protecting you? How does **Psalm 23** make you feel?

_____

_____

_____

_____

_____

_____

_____

_____

_____

_____

_____

_____

_____

_____

_____

_____

_____

Faith

Hebrews 11:1 *Faith shows the reality of what we hope for; it is the evidence of things we cannot see.*

Hebrews 11 lists people from the Old Testament who exhibited faith in God during unknown and trying times. We all respond differently when going through difficult times. God wants us to draw closer to Him and to trust Him to take care of us.

It is tempting to get mad and blame God when grief events happen, but this is when we must resist that urge and lean on our faith instead. Dealing with grief is difficult. That's why we have to press our way through to get to the other side of it.

What Does Faith Look Like?

When you think about **Hebrews 11:1**, what does that mean to you? How do you put your faith into action? Read all of **Hebrews 11**. Whose story stands out to you? Why does that story resonate with you?

_____

_____

_____

_____

_____

_____

_____

_____

_____

_____

_____

_____

_____

Forgiveness

If you are feeling abandoned, have you forgiven your loved one for dying?

Have you forgiven yourself for all the things that you think you should have done to prevent their death or slow it down? Rationally, you know there isn't anything that you could have done. Irrationally, you feel guilt as if their death is your fault. Maybe you feel guilty for the things that you didn't say before they died.

Now, let's work on forgiveness. Let go of that weight! It's holding you down and isn't helping you at all.

While you were grieving, maybe you said some mean things to friends and family members. Exercise forgiveness, let it go.

Maybe people didn't say what you wanted to hear while you were grieving. They can't change the past, and neither can you. Exercise forgiveness, let it go.

Matthew 6:14-15 "If you forgive those who sin against you, your heavenly Father will forgive you. But if you refuse to forgive others, your Father will not forgive your sins."

Are There People Who You Need to Forgive?

Prayerfully, you will be able to release more of your grief, anger, sadness, and pain over time. Are there things that you need to let go of so that they no longer hinder your growth? Remember to add a date to your response; your responses may change over time.

How Will You Respond?

We all respond to grief differently. Some people immediately accept their loved one's death and find a way to continue in life. Others question God or even get mad at God for "taking their loved one." Some people walk away from God completely and blame Him for the person's death.

The scripture tells us that our faith cannot be shaky nor determined by circumstances. 1 **Corinthians 15:58** *So, my dear brothers and sisters, be strong and immovable. Always work enthusiastically for the Lord, for you know that nothing you do for the Lord is ever useless.*

While you're grieving, while you're hurting, do not lose faith in God. Do not lose hope in the Word of God. Know that God hears every prayer, He sees every tear that falls and He does care. He cared when Jesus cried out to Him from the cross. But there was a greater reason for Jesus staying on the cross and dying for our sins. We just may not know the reason for our loved one's death yet. But I am sure of this one thing, no one leaves this earth without God's knowledge. You matter to God!

Matthew 10:29-31 *What is the price of two sparrows—one copper coin? But not a single sparrow can fall to the ground without your Father knowing it. And the very hairs on your head are all numbered. So don't be afraid; you are more valuable to God than a whole flock of sparrows.*

If God is concerned about the many sparrows in the world, then He most certainly is concerned about you!

It is Well
2 Kings 4:8-37

This text tells the story of Prophet Elisha and a woman from Shunem. She is never named, but is referred to as "The Shunnamite Woman."

Each time Elisha visited the city, she would persuade him to have a meal at her house. Over time, she asked her husband to build a room in their house for Elisha to stay in. One day, Elisha asked her servant, Gehazi, to call the Shunammite woman. He asked what he could do for her. She said that she was taken care of. Gehazi mentioned that she didn't have a son, and her husband was old. (This is relevant because sons took care of their mothers after the father's death). Elisha told her that this time the following year, she would be holding a son in her arms. She immediately told him not to get her hopes up like that.

Just as the prophet said, the following year, she had a son. Years later, the boy was out with his father and the harvesters, and he cried out that his head hurt. The father told his servant to take the boy home to his mother. The mother held her son in her lap. The boy died. The Shunammite woman saddled a horse and went to see Elisha. Gehazi saw her coming and met her. He asked, "Is it well with thee?" (King James Version). She responded, "It is well." She didn't stop; she kept riding towards Elisha. She dropped to Elisha's feet and reminded him that she had told him not to get her hopes up about a son. Now her son was dead.

How could a woman who just lost her son say, "It is well." It was not well, her son was dead. Yes, her son died, but her faith did not. She went to see the man of God because the only person who could help her was the man of God.

Elisha immediately saddled up and went to her house. He lay upon the child, mouth to mouth, eyes to eyes, hands to hands. Elisha's body warmed the boy up and God revived the boy to life.

God does not bring everyone back to life. But our faith should not be based on that. Our faith is based on who God is. He is our Creator, regardless of our circumstances. Declare that regardless of what is going on, "It is well."

"It is Well" Declarations

Romans 4:17 *That is what the Scriptures mean when God told him, "I have made you the father of many nations." This happened because Abraham believed in the God who brings the dead back to life and who creates new things out of nothing.* Everything may not be well **yet**, but write it down and declare it now. Use the power of your words.

_____

_____

_____

_____

_____

_____

Self-Assessment

- What triggers my grief (places, people, pictures, items)?

- What can I do to prevent this?

- What helps to relieve my grief? Is it a healthy coping mechanism? If not, how can I make this change?

- Have I communicated my needs to those who are helping (talking, not talking, just being in their presence)?

But if Not

We all pray for God to heal our friends and family. Sometimes He heals them on earth, and sometimes God heals them in heaven. What will you do when the choice is to let them die on earth, and God heals them in heaven? What will you do? Will you get mad and walk away from God? Or will you choose to trust God and remain faithful to Him and His word?

But if not. I took this term from **Daniel 3:18**. This chapter is about Nebuchadnezzar, who built a golden statue that everyone was to bow down to it whenever the music was played. The problem is that God says that His children shall not worship any other god. So the three Hebrew boys, Shadrach, Meshach, and Abednego, refused to bow down.

Nebuchadnezzar threatened to throw them into a burning, fiery furnace. The boys responded that they knew God could save them. The King James Version of **Daniel 3:18** says, "**But if not**, be it known unto thee, O king, that we will not serve thy gods, nor worship the golden image which thou hast set up."

Do you have "**but if not**" faith? If not, do you want it? I believe that you do, or you wouldn't have purchased this journal. You are probably looking for a way to deal with the loss of your loved one. Working on accepting God's decision to heal them in heaven. The fact that this is a struggle is common and ok.

My "But if Not" Declarations

What decision have you made regarding your faith in God? Will you intentionally choose not to let your faith be affected by your grief? What declarations do you need to state to be successful?

_____

_____

_____

_____

_____

_____

_____

_____

_____

_____

_____

_____

_____

_____

Unexplained Trouble

Have you ever wondered, "Why me?" "Why did this happen to me?" In **Job 1**, God asked Satan where he had come from. Satan said that he had been patrolling the earth to see what was going on. God asked Satan if he had noticed His servant Job. God then bragged on Job and said that he was the finest man on all the earth. He avoided evil, operated in integrity, and was without blame (**Job 1:8**). Satan responded and said that was only because God protected him, his home, and his property. And God made him rich, so of course Job lived such a life. But Satan assumed that if God took all of that away, Job would immediately curse God to His face (**Job 1:9–11**).

God then gave Satan permission to test Job by taking away his possessions, but not his life (**Job 1:12**). Satan left to do just that. The rest of chapter one tells how Satan killed all of Job's animals, servants, and his children and destroyed his home. Job tore his robe, covered his head in ashes, and fell to the ground to worship (yes, worship). "I came naked from my mother's womb, and I will be naked when I leave. The LORD gave me what I had, and the LORD has taken it away. Praise the name of the LORD!" (**Job 1:20**). Why me? Why not you?

Can God trust you with trouble? Can God trust you not to blame Him for your pain and walk away? Can God trust you to remain faithful in the midst of your pain?

Job 42 is the last chapter in the book. God restored Job with double what he originally had. You may hear some preachers say, "Job got double for his trouble." But the truth is that in all of Job's suffering, he never cursed God or lost his faith. He maintained his integrity. He even prayed for his friends who accused him of sinning. Can God trust you with trouble?

Have you ever thought, "Why me?" How can you encourage yourself to get through these feelings when they surface?

Miserable Comforters

Have you had a friend or family member say the wrong thing while you're grieving? You know in your heart that they mean well, but it just didn't come out right. What do you do?

The book of Job tells the story of a man who was faithful to God and had been blessed with a wife, children, servants, and livestock. He had everything that he needed.

One day, a conversation between God and Satan took place that would literally change his whole life. Satan was looking for someone to trouble, and God asked him if he had considered Job. (Visit www.youtube.com/@covenantbcc and watch the Bible study videos from May - July 2023 for the study of the book of Job). God presented Job as one who could be tested by Satan and one who would not blame God for his trouble, one who would not curse God for his trouble, and one who would not give up on God because of his trouble.

As a test, Satan killed Job's servants, livestock, and children.

Job's friends came to visit him during his bereavement. The first seven days, they were quiet and just sat with him. Then the accusations of sin began. In chapter 16, Job had had enough, and he said, "I have heard all this before. What miserable comforters you are! (**Job 16:2**)"

You may understand Job's feelings if you've ever had someone say the wrong thing while you're grieving. What is the best way to handle these situations?

I have a couple suggestions for dealing with "miserable comforters."

The first is to give them some grace. There isn't one right thing to say to anyone when they're grieving. And perhaps the person means well, but they are struggling to find the right words.

The second suggestion is to tell the person what you need. It might be to sit with you quietly, maybe take a walk, go to an event, or allow you to express your grief.

Express your feelings of dealing with miserable comforters. Think about how you would like others to express their condolences to you and tell them.

_____

_____

_____

_____

_____

_____

_____

_____

_____

_____

Life Support

Let me start by saying that I am not an expert regarding life support. I am not a medical professional either. I was introduced to life support at the end of my mother's life. I know about life support as a pastor and as a family member. I wanted to include this chapter to hopefully give comfort to those who must make a decision for a loved one regarding life support, as well as to offer comfort to those who have already been through the process. Having a loved one on life support can be grueling, especially when you don't know what your loved one's preference would be.

Allow me to put my pastor hat on and tell you that the decision for that person to live or die does not depend on those machines, the doctors, or you. Machines do what the body cannot. But God is the giver and receiver of life. Please understand that you may give the direction to disconnect the machines, but you are not making the decision of whether your loved one lives or dies. You cannot control the pumping of their hearts or the inhales and exhales of their lungs. You dictate when the machine stops, but the rest of it is up to God.

Do You Have a Friend or Family Member on Life Support?

If you currently have a friend or family member on life support, spend time with them. Hold their hand or rub their arm to let them feel your touch. Talk to them or read to them so they can hear your voice. If you are on the other side of dealing with someone on life support, I extend to you my condolences.

Write. It can be about how you're feeling, if you are struggling or have already been through this situation. It can be to your loved one, or to a friend who is grieving. Write.

_____

_____

_____

_____

_____

_____

_____

_____

_____

_____

_____

Preparing to Say Goodbye

There are a couple of different opportunities here. One is that you can begin to say the things that you want to say (I love you, I'm sorry, I appreciate you for...).

Preparing to say goodbye is also an opportunity to prepare yourself to life without having your loved one in your life. Your preparation may be emotional, financial, logistical, or even spiritual. This preparation is a part of the acceptance that your loved one is going to die.

When you have a loved one with a terminal illness, or maybe it's someone who isn't expected to make it, it can be an opportunity to say all the things that you want to say before they die.

The day before my mother died, she was in a coma. I didn't know that it was ok (or even encouraged) to speak to her. But when my father died 30 years later, I did speak to him and hold his hand in his unconscious state.

My Thoughts About Saying "Goodbye"

- What are your fears as you deal with your loved one dying?
- If your loved one has already passed, what fears did you have and how did/are you dealing with them?
- What are your plans for accepting life without your loved one?

The First of Firsts

The first Christmas, birthday, anniversary, family reunion, or vacation without your loved one can be hard and very emotional. We immediately think of traditions that will never be the same because our loved ones are gone. The first of firsts. The person who used to carve the turkey might be gone, or the one who used to bake the cakes, or maybe it's the one who used to organize the vacations. And the first event without them may feel empty. These can be challenging times, and it's normal to feel that way. My recommendation is for you to prepare for it before the day comes. You cannot predict your feelings on that day, but you can prepare yourself for it.

Consider creating a plan ahead of time of how you would like to handle that day (one day/event at a time). Would you like to spend it with loved ones? Would you like to look at old pictures or home movies? How would you like to deal with your grief on that day?

An important thing to remember is that it is OK to be OK. It's OK to laugh and experience joy on that day. It's OK to enjoy your life! That does not diminish the love you have for your loved one. It does not diminish their memory. My father and I loved my mother. But we chose not to spend the first Christmas crying because we missed her. If you have made it through your first of firsts, congratulations. Not everyone makes it, but you did.

Preparation for the First of the Firsts

How do you plan to acknowledge the first event without your loved one? What is your plan to honor their memory but not make you feel sad?

_____

_____

_____

_____

_____

_____

_____

_____

_____

_____

_____

_____

_____

_____

_____

Nobody Cares!

Do you ever feel like you're in this alone? Nobody cares that you're grieving. Nobody cares that your loved one died. The funeral is over; everyone went home. Nobody cares! Everyone has moved on with their life, but you're still hurting, and nobody cares!

Thinking that nobody cares is a legitimate feeling, but it may not be reality. When we are hurting, we feel like no one else knows how we feel. It's easy to feel like you're the only person who has ever dealt with death like this. It might sincerely feel that way, but it's not true. That's why there are so many different types of grief counselors, groups, and books to help you deal with grief. The good news is that you are not alone.

Yes, people do care about your grief. But we are all human and limited in our ability to express that love and care sometimes. Even at the most important moments of your life, people will seemingly fail you. But do not give up. Maybe today isn't a good day for them to share in your grief but tomorrow might be better.

Maybe that person is still dealing with their own grief and they cannot talk about it yet. Keep searching to find a person or group who can help. And extend a little grace to those who do care but are unable to help right now.

You might **feel** like nobody cares, but God does.

Does Anybody Care? My Thoughts

- Reflect on why you feel like nobody cares about your grief.
- Have you misinterpreted someone's words or actions?
- How will you handle your grief?

Suicide is Not the Answer

If you are not OK, please let someone know. Don't wait for someone to figure it out. Don't wait for everyone to notice that you're having a hard time. It may not be as obvious as you think.

After a person commits suicide, we see the videos of their confused family and friends saying, "I just saw them," or "I just talked to them." That person did not know that their friend or loved one was struggling and on the edge. Again, the signs may not be as obvious as you think.

Please do not suffer in silence. There is help available every day, all day, 24/7/365.

Call or text 988 from anywhere in the United States. You can even chat with them on their website, https://988lifeline.org.

"At the 988 Suicide & Crisis Lifeline, we understand that life's challenges can sometimes be difficult. Whether you're facing mental health struggles, emotional distress, alcohol or drug use concerns, or just need someone to talk to, our caring counselors are here for you. You are not alone."*

Here are some other resources:
- Veterans Crisis Line: Call 988, then press 1 or text 838255
- Substance Abuse and Mental Health Services Administration (SAMHSA): 800-662-4357
- Crisis Text Line: Text HOME to 741-741 in the U.S.27
- Please read Suicide Help (https://www.helpguide.org/mentalhealth/suicide-self-harm/are-you-feeling-suicidal), talk to someone you trust, or call a suicide helpline:
- In the U.S., call 1-800-273-8255.
- In the UK, call 08457 90 90 90.
- In Australia, call 13 11 14.
- Or visit IASP (https://findahelpline.com/i/iasp) to find a helpline in your country.*

You matter! There is help available for you. Suicide is not the answer!

*Accessed March 16, 2025, https://988lifeline.org/.

*Melinda Smith, Lawrence Robinson, Jeanne Segal, "Coping with Grief and Loss," accessed March 26, 2025, https://www.helpguide.org/mental-health/grief/coping-with-grief-and-loss.

Don't Suffer in Silence

Have you ever considered suicide? What prevented you from following through? What is your plan for the next time you feel this way? Do you have a friend or family member who is a victim of suicide? How does that make you feel?

Survivor's Guilt

Have you ever felt guilty for living after your loved one died? God called your loved one home, you feel like they were a better person than you, but they're gone and you're still here. Maybe you were both in an accident, they died and you survived. Survivor's Guilt is real. "Survivor's guilt is the response to an event that some people experience when they survive a traumatic event or situation that others did not."*

Please do not allow guilt to rob you of the life you have left. Please get help, whether professionally or socially, but do not suffer in silence. God left you here for a reason. We cannot always understand God's ways, but we must always trust Him.

My Thoughts

_____

_____

_____

_____

_____

_____

_____

_____

_____

*Bistas, K., & Grewal, R. (2023). The Intricacies of Survivor's Guilt: Exploring Its Phenomenon Across Contexts. Cureus, 15(9), e45703. https://doi.org/10.7759/cureus.45703.

Accepting Changes

With every loss, there will be a change. Change is not always easy to accept. Sometimes the change is a house that is so quiet that it feels so loud. You can hear every move you make, unlike when other people are in the house.

The change may be in your routine. Maybe you were a caregiver, and now you have to try to remember what you did before that. Maybe your loss was a job. How do you fill your days now? You might feel overwhelmed, but I promise that it will get better. Please don't give up on yourself to survive, and don't give up on God.

Proverbs 3:5-6 *Trust in the LORD with all your heart; do not depend on your own understanding. Seek his will in all you do, and he will show you which path to take.*

What does this scripture mean to you? What change(s) are you experiencing? How are you going to exercise your trust God?

_____

_____

_____

_____

_____

_____

_____

Self-Assessment

- How do I feel today?

- Do I feel like I'm moving forward, backward, or not at all?

- Am I OK with that today?

How to Move Beyond Grief

Grief can be emotionally demanding. It can uncover the insecurity of being alone or the dependencies that we had on our loved ones. And socially it's such a change that it takes time to adjust. "Grieving is the process of working through grief. Providers who help people cope with grief use words like 'working' or 'moving' through grief to highlight the demands grief places on us."*

I'll be honest, working or moving through grief is work; however, the benefits will outweigh the effort. You will grow stronger and find yourself being able to process other life events in a different way. "Working through difficult emotions can give you the strength you need to move forward in your life while continuing to hold a place in your heart for the loved ones and life experiences you've lost."*

Do you feel like you would be dishonoring your loved one if you moved past your grief? You're not. Do you feel like it is a badge of honor to hold on to this grief? It's not. When you live in a state of grief, you are robbing everyone else of yourself and the joy that you bring to their lives. And what about you? You deserve to have a bountiful life, in spite of the loss that you've suffered.

So, how long is too long to mourn and grieve? There isn't a definitive answer. Unfortunately, the only way to get through grief is by going through it. What is the proper way to grieve?

*"Grief," last reviewed February 22, 2023, https://my.clevelandclinic.org/health/diseases/24787-grief.

There aren't any rules for this either. Well, I have one rule: you cannot grieve forever.

Guilt can be associated with grief—guilt about being ready to move beyond your grief, guilt about being OK, guilt about being alive and being ready to live your life when your loved one can't. Moving beyond grief does not mean forgetting your loved one. It does not mean that you don't care. Moving beyond grief means not allowing grief to envelop your life. It is an acceptance of the death and your decision to live. Moving beyond grief is finding healthy ways to deal with your grief and accepting that it's OK to be OK. You are not obligated to grieve or mourn for any certain period of time. Do not allow others to make you feel guilty for being OK.

Society tries to place rules on widows. But legally and biblically, the marital obligation ends with the death of the spouse. When or if a man or woman should remarry is their personal decision. Children cannot take the place of a spouse, and living alone is not easy for everyone.

Moving beyond grief doesn't have to be an isolated process. Please do not suffer in silence. If you aren't comfortable expressing your grief with a friend or family member, then find an outside, unrelated source. "Men tend to have worse depression and more health problems than women do after the loss. Some researchers think this may be because men tend to have less social support after a loss." The internet can be a great source to find a virtual group if you don't want to meet in

*"Grief, Bereavement, and Loss (PDQ®)–Patient Version," accessed March 27, 2025, https://www.cancer.gov/about-cancer/advanced-cancer/caregivers/planning/bereavement-pdq.

person. Or you might want to discover a new group with similar interests. I found a book club and a women's group online.

Will grief ever go away? Yes and no. Hopefully for everyone, the intensity of grief will change over time. I don't grieve for any of my family members anymore. I still love and miss them. But it's rare that I cry about the loss now. When I started writing this book, I was shocked by how many tears I shed. The grief had not gone away. It was tough reaching back to those feelings from the initial loss, but I wanted to be authentic in my writing. My grief is not front and center, but this book proves that it isn't gone forever either.

Why is grief so hard? Because you lost a loved one, a spouse, a friend, or a pet; you lost a piece of your heart. It's a loss because a part of your life has been permanently altered. Perhaps that loss affects your identity. And now you're trying to figure out who you are without that person.

We will always miss our loved ones. But over time, grief becomes manageable and less prevalent. The tears will eventually turn to smiles, and with happy memories.

How do you know if you've moved beyond grief? Although we never completely stop grieving, there are signs that we've moved beyond it and are living a life not dominated by grief. For example, there were times that I would write something, and then when I read it, I was shocked. I realized that I had buried that memory, but my subconscious brought it to the forefront as I typed. I have my memories; I never remained in a sad state of life.

Don't Stay in the State You're In

In the book, I talked about a funeral that I officiated. There were many friends and family coming in from multiple states. If everyone stayed in their current state, they would never make it to the funeral. They literally had to change states in order to get there.

That's like grief. We cannot stay in a state of grief and think that we will reach the desired destination. In order to progress through your grief, you have to keep moving towards the goal of healing. Some days you may move fast like a plane, other days you might move slower like a bus. But as long as you keep moving (i.e., working), you will make progress and move out of the state of grief.

Are You Feeling Anxious or Angry?

Write. Don't allow those feelings to build up. The more you focus on them, the greater the feelings become. Write them down and release them.

How I Plan to Move Beyond My Grief

How will you move beyond your grief? What markers will you use to let you know that you're making progress? Will your determination be based on time? Or will you focus on your response to different events (not being upset by certain events, able to return to certain events, willing to do various events)?

Strengthen What Remains

Revelation 3:2 *Wake up! Strengthen what little remains, for even what is left is almost dead. I find that your actions do not meet the requirements of my God.*

Instead of looking at what you lost, focus on what remains. Look at what you still have. You still have something to be grateful for in your life. That might be in a friend or family member, your job, housing, or food. Surviving one day at a time is a strength. Maintaining your sanity is a strength. What will you choose to focus on?

_____

_____

_____

_____

_____

_____

_____

_____

_____

_____

Allow God to Lead

Psalm 37:23-24 *The LORD directs the steps of the godly. He delights in every detail of their lives. Though they stumble, they will never fall, for the LORD holds them by the hand.*

Allowing God to lead means praying about your heart's desires. But not implementing anything until you receive a confirmation from the Lord. That confirmation may come to you in prayer, while reading the Word, or through a message from your pastor. Some people have dreams or visions from the Lord for direction.

I pray that you will seek the Lord for guidance while you're grieving and afterward.

How Will You Let God Lead?

_____

_____

_____

_____

_____

_____

_____

Heaven and Heavenly Things

A question that I get asked a lot is, "Is heaven real?" I believe that it is (**Revelation 21:1–2**). From the Old to the New Testament, God gives us comfort in knowing that all who are in Christ will see their loved ones again.

If you are in Christ, meaning that you are saved, and your loved one was also in Christ, then you will see each other again in heaven. **First Thessalonians 4:13–14** promises, "And now, dear brothers and sisters, we want you to know what will happen to the believers who have died so you will not grieve like people who have no hope. For since we believe that Jesus died and was raised to life again, we also believe that when Jesus returns, God will bring back with him the believers who have died." I often say that we are not "like people who have no hope." That's why I know that the death of a loved one is not supposed to make us want to give up on life. We will be reunited again. This is a common scripture quoted during funerals because it is a message of hope.

Another question that I get a lot is whether we will know our loved ones in heaven. I believe the answer is yes. In **Luke 16:19–31**, Jesus tells the parable of the rich man and Lazarus (not the same Lazarus who was raised from the dead). The rich man lived lavishly and dressed in fine linens. Lazarus was a beggar; his body was covered in sores, and he lay at the gate of the rich man every day. He longed to be fed from the rich man's crumbs. One day, Lazarus died. The angels carried him to Abraham's side.

The rich man also died, and he was buried. While in hell, the rich man looked up and saw Lazarus from afar by Abraham's side. He begged Father Abraham to allow Lazarus to dip his finger in water and cool his tongue because he was in agony.

Jesus used this parable to show us that there is life after this, whether one is in heaven or hell. I believe it also proves that we will recognize one another in heaven. The rich man knew who Lazarus was on earth, but he had never seen Abraham, yet he knew who Abraham was. (I didn't finish telling you the story on purpose. I hope you're intrigued enough to go read it, Luke 16:19–3.)

At funerals, we offer words of comfort. For those who are saved, these scriptures are comforting. For those who aren't saved, it can be a reminder that tomorrow is not promised. After death, there are no second chances to get to heaven. Today is a good day for salvation!

What are your thoughts on heaven and the opportunity to see your loved one(s) again?

_____

_____

_____

_____

_____

_____

How to Find a Church Home

When you are selecting a church home, think about what's important to you. Do you want a pastor who explains the scriptures or gives a high-level overview? Do you want a church with families like yours? Are you looking for one that has a daycare, a singles' ministry, a widows' group, or a young adult group? If you have no clue, that's not a problem. You can learn a lot from the church website.

If you are nervous about going to the church, watching the service online can help you become familiar with the order of service and how they worship. That helps to decrease some of the anxiety. It will also give you some familiarity with the pastor's style of preaching. It can be intimidating going to a new church, especially if you're doing it alone like I was. But I pray that you will find a friendly church home where you can learn, grow stronger in Christ, and make friends.

There are churches that have small groups where you get to know some of the church members on a more intimate level. I love Bible study and Sunday school because you can ask questions in class and sometimes share your story. Having a church home is like having a community. There are usually people at different stages in their relationship with Christ. Some may not have accepted Jesus as their Savior yet, some may have been out of church for years, some may have just walked in a church for the first time. I have been in all three of these stages. And of course, there are the established Christians who are there to help others.

As a pastor, I hope that your emphasis is on the Word (the scriptures from the Bible) that is being preached, but I understand that we all have different desires. And while I have your attention, please allow me to plead on behalf of smaller churches. Please don't ignore the church that doesn't have all the groups or ministries that you're looking for. As the church begins to grow, those things can be added. Focus on what will nourish your spiritual soul. Does the Word that's being preached speak to you? Does it inspire you to learn more and want to live a holy life?

However you select your church home does not matter. I just hope that you find one. God will give you a confirmation that you are right where you're supposed to be.

How to Pick a Bible Translation

When you are looking for a Bible, find a translation that you can understand. Some common versions are: King James Version (KJV), New International Version (NIV), and New Living Translation (NLT).

I preach from the KJV, but I could not understand it when I first started going to church. It has a lot of th's in it: thee, thou, hither, goeth, doeth, liveth. But somehow over time, I began to understand it. The NIV and NLT translations are easier to read and understand than KJV. The scripture quotations in this book are from NLT, unless otherwise stated. Look at 1 Corinthians 13 and see which translation you prefer, and then purchase that Bible.

I am the founding pastor of **Covenant Believers Community Church.** You're welcome to view our services on Facebook Live or YouTube Live on Sundays at 11:00 am ET and Wednesdays at 6:30 p.m. ET. If you're ever in Columbus, Ohio, on a Sunday morning, please join us for service.

Have You Accepted Jesus Christ as Your Savior?

Do you know what it means to accept Jesus as your savior?

Romans 10:9-13

9If you openly declare that Jesus is Lord and believe in your heart that God raised him from the dead, you will be saved. 10For it is by believing in your heart that you are made right with God, and it is by openly declaring your faith that you are saved. 11As the Scriptures tell us, "Anyone who trusts in him will never be disgraced." 12Jew and Gentile are the same in this respect. They have the same Lord, who gives generously to all who call on him. 13For "Everyone who calls on the name of the LORD will be saved."

Jesus desires to have a relationship with us. **Revelation 3:20** *"Look! I stand at the door and knock. If you hear my voice and open the door, I will come in, and we will share a meal together as friends.*

Baptism

Mark 1:9-11

9One day Jesus came from Nazareth in Galilee, and John baptized him in the Jordan River. 10As Jesus came up out of the water, he saw the heavens splitting apart and the Holy Spirit descending on him̲ like a dove. 11And a voice from heaven said, "You are my dearly loved Son, and you bring me great joy."

Acts 2:38

Peter replied, "Each of you must repent of your sins and turn to God, and be baptized in the name of Jesus Christ for the forgiveness of your sins. Then you will receive the gift of the Holy Spirit.

Romans 6:3-4

3Or have you forgotten that when we were joined with Christ Jesus in baptism, we joined him in his death? 4For we died and were buried with Christ by baptism. And just as Christ was raised from the dead by the glorious power of the Father, now we also may live new lives.

Salvation, Baptism, Church Home

Are you saved? Do you have a desire to be saved? If you are saved, has grief shaken or strengthened your foundation in Christ?

Have you been baptized? Is that important to you? Most churches do not require membership for baptism. If you would like to get baptized, please ask them about the process.

Do you have a church home? Is that important to you? Do you have a desire to be a part of a faith community? How ill you find a church home?

Other Products by Keia Holt:

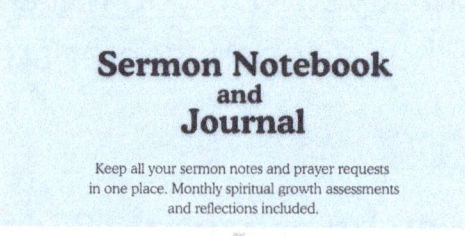

Dealing with Grief and How to Move Beyond It

Sermon Notebook and Journal

www.keiaholt.com

www.amazon.com/ author/keia.holt

Did you enjoy this Guided Journal?

Please leave a review on Amazon to help others who may be considering this journal.

https://www.amazon.com/author/keia.holt

Keia K Holt: books, biography, latest update

Follow Keia K Holt and explore their bibliography from Amazon's Keia K Holt Author Page.

a Amazon.com

I pray that you have been blessed by this journal.

We may have connected because of our grief, but I pray that this connection will grow beyond that. Please follow me on Facebook, Instagram, Threads, and/or TikTok.

You are a seed that was buried. Now it's time to grow.

Keia K. Holt, Author